MEMORIES OF
CRABBE STREET NO.29
1950 – 1963

*To Jackie and Linda
With love
from
Pat
x x*

By Pat Ward
Aldeburgh, Suffolk

**MEMORIES OF LITTLE HOUSE
IN CRABBE STREET NO.29
1950 – 1963**

2020 Edition

First printed and Published 2005
by Leiston Press
Unit 1 - 1b
Masterlord Industrial Estate
Leiston
Suffolk
IP16 4JD

Copyright © Pat Ward

All rights reserved. No part of this publication may be reproduced, stored in a retrieval system, or transmitted in any form or by any means, without the prior consent of Pat Ward.

Proceeds go to Aldeburgh Jubilee Hall

ISBN 978-1-911311-74-4

ACKNOWLEDGEMENTS

Deborah Crow – Administration
Mr and Mrs John James – Aldeburgh Book Shop
Mr Brian E Ward – Photos
Mr Bob Burns – Flood Photo The Baggott Family – Photo
Mrs P Ewer – Photo
Lindy Allfrey – The Cross Keys Painting
Ann Bye - Wards Garage Photo
Peter Harris - Christmas "Buffs" Party Photo
Maurice Smith - Aldeburgh Lifeboat 1957 Photo
Derek Johnson - Railway Garden
Dr A. Jones- 'Rats' Mower Photo
Tony Husband - Cartoon Sketch

Front cover:
Pat and Margaret outside No.29 Crabbe Street, August,1958

Back cover:
The Cross Keys by Lindy Allfrey (once a Crabbe Street Resident)

For my son Nick
and dedicated to
my late parents,
Brian (Pixie) and Colleen, 'Carnival Legends'
and brother Richard
and all the local people past
and present I grew up with.

1

I was born at Patrick Stead Hospital, Halesworth, on 25th January, 1950.

I was told that my father (Brian) came over to the hospital to see Mum (Colleen) and me, on a very icy evening, on the back of Uncle Spud Murphy's motorbike. They had to go so slow that by the time they got there it was five minutes before ward closing. Dad arrived with some flowers that looked rather worse for wear, but Mum was still pleased to see him! When they got back to Aldeburgh they just made it five minutes before closing time at the pub!

My parents wanted a son called Patrick. The nurses at the hospital thought I should be called 'Snowdrop' as I was born when they were just coming out, but in the end my parents settled on Patricia Ann.

29 Crabbe Street was my first home and here began my memories of that tiny little house by the sea.

1 My uncle had a new baby boy, Christopher, who was also born there a few days before me on 17th January,
2 The motorbike was an old Army Communication Dispatch rider's bike, a 250cc. It had an old iron carrier on the back for paper work.

2

At the age of eight months, I was told that my mother had always put me in my pram on the pavement outside the house, to get fresh air and on one particular day when she went to bring me in she was unable to wake me. When I woke up I was screaming and I held my left leg up in the air so my parents phoned the doctor from the post office phone box and he immediately came to the house. It was Dr Robin and he stated that I would need to go to Ipswich hospital. I was diagnosed with Osteomyelitis which is a disease of the hip bone. I was placed on the danger list for six weeks. It took a few weeks for me to recover after having antibiotics. The doctors told my parents that I wouldn't be able to walk until I was five years old.

I was told that I always moved to the music in my cot when the radio came on. Then at eighteen months I walked! My mother took me to the consultant and proudly stated that Patricia could walk. "Nonsense", the consultant replied, "the child can't walk she's had Osteomyelitis". My mother said, "She can". His reply was "show me the child". My mother placed me down on the ground with my new shoes on and I walked tottering along. "Amazing", the consultant said and scratched his head.

Note: Years later I was told that my Great-grandfather Ward had also had the disease, which caused him to have a club foot.

"Snooks"
Aldeburgh's famous dog.
Owned by Doctor Robin and Nora Acheson.
He often accompanied them on their visits.

Flood
Crabbe Street looking South towards No.29 - The 1953 Flood

3
1953

My first memory of life was at the age of three, in Crabbe Street,[3] during the winter of 1953. I looked out from my bedroom window and asked, "Where are the cars, why are there boats in the street?" The sea had come over and we were completely flooded, as were many coastal areas of England.

We stayed at my grandparents Jack and Elsie Murphys' house in Leiston until the water subsided, and we were ready to come back to live a few months later. The people of Canada gave families a beautiful carpet to help flood victims and we got one. We always saw the tidemark on the sitting room walls, as it would come through the wallpaper every time they wallpapered! This happened even years after the floods.

Probably my second memory was connected to the sea. One cold, stormy winter's night, the Lifeboat gun went off about midnight. Dad promptly rushed to the Lifeboat station (it was the routine in those days, when the gun went off, many of the local men who were able, would rush to get there first, as it was a way of earning a few shillings, first come, first served). So it was a real rush of excitement to see them all run down to the beach. Dad got to the Lifeboat, and Mum and I stood on the beach, both of us in our nighties watching. We waved them off, but we were concerned if they would return safely, as it was a wild old night. I loved to watch the return of the Lifeboat, because the men would walk around in a circle each pushing a pole to winch up the boat from the sea. There were such lovely strong men doing this, like Ruben Woods and Johnny Burrell.

---

3   Our house was more or less a gift from Grandfather Ward, who gave the house as a wedding present to my parents. It was my first home.

4
1954

One day while playing outside the house on the pavement (we of course, didn't have a garden, only a yard about two feet wide, so the pavement and the beach were my playground), I happened to spot a parade of young girls going into the Jubilee Hall two by two, each with a ballet dress and shoes on their arms. I instantly decided to go along too, and do the same. So I went up stairs, got my pillowcase off my pillow, placed it over my arm, got my black plimsolls, then carried them in my hands in the same way and ran in behind them. They were all gathered around on stage, the girls were having make-up put on them, and when they started to put some on me one exclaimed, "Hey! wait a minute, we don't know you little girl, what are you doing here?". I promptly replied, "I want to dance!" The reply was, "But you can't little girl, you don't know the dances!" They asked where I lived, I pointed, and then someone took me to my house. When my mother opened the door, they said "I think she wants to dance!" My parents then sent me to ballet classes.

---

4 I was at a history group meeting in 2014 to hear a talk by a Rona Newson about her ballet career. I asked her if she had taught ballet in Aldeburgh in 1955 at the bottom of the Town Steps as her face looked familiar. She said she had and I told her that she had taught me. She told me she could remember me and that I was attentive, which is amazing, as I am quite a fidget! Rona studied ballet in London with Audrey Hepburn which is as close as I'll ever get to fame!

5 Mum took me once, to a social evening, when I was about six years old at the Aldeburgh Young People's Club on Victoria Road. I was keen to dance and asked if I could dance on the stage. The kind gentleman put on Swan Lake for me. I was in heaven.

Pat dressed for Ballet, 1954

5

On 30th November, 1954, at Patrick Stead Hospital, Halesworth, my dear sister Margaret Susan (the second child) was born. She was a lovely dear sister, so pretty. I was so proud of her, and if anyone said anything about her, I would say, "She's *my* sister". Dad didn't visit the hospital on the old army motorbike this time!

Margaret was a very sociable child, outgoing and a real smiler. In those days in that little back street, because we didn't have a yard big enough, Mum would put little Margaret in her wooden high chair out in the front on the pavement to eat her food. She would stop people to chat and smile to passers-by, and everyone admired her.

I can remember when she was about three my parents put her in the Carnival as a 'doll in a box', she really did look like a beautiful little doll.

6

1955

One day, while walking down from Nana and Grandad Wards' house (101 Saxmundham Road), my mother and I with Margaret in the pram, came to where the railway station was on Victoria Road. Upon seeing the beautiful railway garden on the opposite side of the road, I decided to get a closer look. Not mentioning to my mother that I wished to do that, I proceeded to cross the road, whereby immediately I came into a collision with a car, which knocked me down. I arrived under the bonnet! Then scooting myself up out from under the car, I wiped a little blood off my forehead, and exclaimed, "Phew!" The poor driver was a wreck and my mother stood there in shock. I don't know what Dad said to my mother afterwards, or even if she dared tell him about it.

Billy Botterill who was porter at Aldeburgh Station from 1921 until closure in 1966. Bill took great pride in caring for the station's gardens.

7

1956 ONWARDS

As we lived so near to the cinema and considering how much I loved singing and dancing, I was very lucky to be able to visit the "pictures", as often as I could. Around the age of six or seven and from then on, I would craze my Dad for a shilling so I could go to the pictures on my own. There I would be right on the front row in the middle, to take in all the fabulous Hollywood films. After seeing a film, I would copy all the singing and dancing that I had seen and everyone would see me singing and dancing up and down the streets for a week, until the next one was seen.

There was a double billing every Sunday night and there were always queues. I really enjoyed Calamity Jane (Doris Day), Carousel, Seven Brides for Seven Brothers, The King and I (Yul Brynner), The Parent Trap (Hayley Mills), etc, etc. May I add that the pictures was my early courting place, for a good kiss in the back row. I spent half my life in the Aldeburgh pictures. It was my life – and still is.

8

APPROX. 1956 UNTIL 1958

Whilst playing on the seafront one day, it started to rain, so I went for cover under a bay window of Ocean House. Suddenly I heard tapping on the window behind me. To my surprise it was two little girls and their mother beckoning me to come in. I went round, they opened the door and I went in. To my amazement we laughed and talked but we couldn't understand each other! They were speaking German (as the mother was German) and I of course English. These two girls became my great friends, Connie and Sylvia Ballou (their father was an American based at RAF Bentwaters; obviously, he had met his wife whilst stationed in Germany).

We spent hours playing together and I visited them all the time. I loved their toys and cosy house. We taught each other our languages. I learnt to count in German and learn some phrases, which I never forgot. On one of my birthdays, their mother bought me the most beautiful American dress, which was tartan and had a red vest and tartan sleeves. I was the happiest child getting that dress! One of the funniest phrases one of them came out with, which my father especially enjoyed and we never forgot it, was when my brother Richard was born in the house. The girls were told and came to see him, and one of them asked, "Where did you get the baby?" and was told, "The stork brought it". Her reply was, "But how did da stork get in da vindow?" Great laughter by all and my father always laughed at this.

9

1956

'Connie' lived in Oakley Square, with her husband and little boy. Connie told us she came from Bald Eagle, Tennessee, USA, and she said her 'Daddy' was the Chief Hog Caller! Mum and her best friend Beatie Fowlger ('Beat' as we called her), became friends with Connie. Mum and Beat couldn't help but chuckle when they would see Connie arriving on the beach, just as they would be leaving at the end of the day. She would be carrying her little transistor radio under her arm and reminded me of the character 'Olive Oil', because she was so thin. One day Connie's husband took her to London to buy her a new dress. That same evening opposite us Mum, Dad, Beat and friends were in the Cross Keys pub having a drink, when Connie came in. She proudly announced, "Here I am, I'm all dressed up, and I got my hand bag to match, when I get back to Bald Eagle I'll be the best dressed gal there!" They asked her, "Connie what would you like to drink?" she said, "I'll have a Guynesse!"

Down the street, almost opposite the yacht pond at No.13, lived another American family whom Mum got to know. The wife was Japanese and she had two children. Mum often visited her (name unknown). One day Mum asked her if she would like to have more children. She exclaimed, "Ah! No, me catcha no more babies!"

Valerie Foulger, Margaret and the little American boy outside Connie's House, Oakley Square

Beat and Mum outside The Cross Keys.

Richard aged 3 on The Cross Keys wall.

10

1957

Richard was born at '29' on 17th June, 1957 (the flags were out as it was the Festival).

Dad had been extending the house (as there were more of us coming) and it took many years to build on the back, both floors. When we first lived there, the stairs were right in front of the door as you came in. So when Mum brought the pram in, she had to manoeuvre very carefully backwards and forwards to get it in. Dad decided to take the stairs out of that position and place them at the back of the house, leading from the sitting room (which gave more room in what was a tiny kitchen). We only had a toilet in the house, no bathroom for many years (actually just before we moved) and I was bathed in a tin bath in front of the fire until I was about twelve.

So whilst the stairs were out we had to go up to bed on a ladder. Great fun for small children! When it was time for Richard to be born the house was still being renovated. Upstairs the floors were not finished and there were just joists to walk across (and the new upstairs bathroom was in construction too). When the midwife came to deliver the baby, she had to climb up the ladder with her bag (Dad behind, I expect, with a kettle of hot water). When she had delivered the baby and was about to leave, she said, "What ever you do, don't let the baby fall down the hole!"

11

Being so close to the beach and loving the sea I had the idea from somewhere that I wanted to throw a bottle into the sea with my name and address on it to see if anyone would find it and reply back. So Dad helped me write a letter and placed it inside a bottle. It read something like. "whoever finds this please write to me". I was a very excited seven years old. So Dad and I walked down to the beach, hand in hand, and threw the bottle into the sea. A short while later, to my amazement, I received a letter from a young man in Holland. It was read out at school and I wrote back. It was the simple things in life that gave me such pleasure.

12

From the early age of about seven, it was my job almost every year on Christmas Eve to go over to Leiston on the bus to deliver all the Christmas presents to my Murphy relatives. I would catch the 6 o'clock bus and carry a big suitcase full of presents to give out. I'd start first at the bottom part of Leiston at Roberts Road at Auntie Josie and Uncle Ron Howard's house. They in return would give me our presents to take home. I would proceed up to St. Margaret's Crescent, first to Uncle Spud and Auntie Nora's, then Grandad and Nana Murphys' house, Auntie Kathleen's, and finally to Auntie Eileen and Uncle Marian Silberts' house, 90 St Margaret's Crescent. It was a lovely task and I felt so welcome and loved. They would say, "Here comes our little Father Christmas, Pat". I would catch the last bus home, and was thrilled to come back with all our presents. Then I would arrive back excited and ready to hang my stocking up!

The most fabulous of Christmas parties were held at Eileen and Marian's house. Marian would pick us all up Christmas night in his car. We would be all dressed up. When we got there all the Murphys were there, it was great. Mum had ten brothers and sisters, so the house was full. All my cousins were of a similar age and we were all friends with each other. We would have fun games, where all ages joined in. There would be music, dancing and singing. I was always asked to do a dance and from the age of four years I would do what I called my Snake Dance. I had scarves, which I used to wear around my waist or dance with. They all wondered where this idea came from, because we didn't have television then. I can still do the dance! They were magic nights over there and the house was so alive and happy. There would be the biggest of Christmas trees which reached the ceiling and was decorated with real lit candles. We believe Marian did a bit of scrumping in the woods!

Grandad Murphy was an excellent dancer (he was Irish, and born in Co. Kildare, Southern Ireland). He had the most wonderful smile, which lit up his whole face and he had a real gleam in his eye. He would place me on his knee and give the tightest of hugs. (He always did this every time he saw me). I loved the way he always kept his cap on, it was his trade mark (see photo).

All of us entertained somehow. Garry (Eileen and Marian's youngest son) did some funny skits with jokes and tricks, and there were often distant relatives from Ireland there too. I was lucky that my cousins were also my best friends, like Linda and 'Scott', who continued to be so for many, many years to come. St Margaret's Crescent should have been called St. Nicholas Crescent, because their house was a 'magical' Christmas house!

Grandad Murphy

13

The most wonderful memories in No.29 were of Carnival time. The whole street came alive and the atmosphere was fantastic. My first Carnival entry was at the age of four years. It was called "Friday Night is Bath Night". How amusing now, to think of one night of the week to bath! That was how it was in 1954.

I was pushed in a hand made cart, with wheels from my old pram, or some body's pram, by Carol Mower, who was draped in a towel. I sat merrily blowing bubbles. This cart was decorated with heather and coloured paper and there were two Union Jacks placed proudly at the front. Looks as if we got a consolation prize. From then on I've been dressed up in the Carnival nearly every year to this present day!

Dad made our house a 'Carnival House', because he decorated it up for the competitions and entered it into the evening illuminations competition. We would eagerly watch opposite ours at the Keys to see their entry and they ours. The sounds of the hammers and saws, and discussions of where to put this or that, the chatter of onlookers and the children's faces smiling, made the atmosphere so exciting, very high. Most all of our relatives from Leiston would come down to our house on the day, and enjoy all the fun. Mum would serve teas in the afternoon when the procession finished. The house entries for Carnivals were many. Dad once created and decorated a little Chinese house, beside it was a bridge and cherry tree. The night time illumination on this was spectacular (see photo).

Another entry was "Somewhere over the Rainbow", for which both Mum and Dad made loads of paper flowers and placed them right across the house to make the rainbow. Dad also made a marvellous replica of the Aldeburgh Crest, a large boat and mast, which stood proudly on a platform; his carpentry skills came in very handy.

Carol Mower and Pat at the Carnival, 1954
"Friday Night is Bath Night"

Chinese House

One of the best entries was called 'The O.K. Corral', a cowboy saloon bar. Dad took off the front door and made two swinging doors to go in its place. The two bottom windows were covered over with original stained glass windows with BAR signs on. There was a hitching post in front and many 'Wanted Dead or Alive' signs. A pair of buffalo horns were placed over the front doorway. It really was the part. They played music inside, so it sounded and looked just like a real cowboy saloon. No wonder then, that in the evening, some of the band, who played in the Carnival, came walking in thinking it was a real pub. They came straight into the kitchen, and one exclaimed, "Ee by gum i'n't it somebody's parlour!"

"The O.K. Corral".
Left to right, Margaret sitting on hitching post, Pat Strowger, Mum, Pat, Richard and Grandad (Charles E Ward),
far left Gail Strowger

Note: My Great Grandfather Ward instigated the Aldeburgh Carnival in the late 1920's. My grandparents would hold an annual fancy dress party on their lawn at the house named 'Colward' on The Terrace. Many local people would peer over the fence and watch. It was decided that everyone should dress up and the Carnival was created. They first called it the Aldeburgh Regatta. A family member, Clifford Butcher, was the first Carnival Prince, and next Burt Ward was dressed up as King Neptune and came out of the sea. Throughout these years, our family has entered in the Carnival almost every year. After we all grew up, Mum and Dad entered in as a comical couple for over twenty years. Lizzy became a Carnival Queen in 1983. On the 60th anniversary of the Carnival Dad made a giant replica of the Crown, and placed the original Crown underneath that the King had worn, and we placed some of the hundreds of photos from years gone by around the float. We all dressed in costumes from previous years and it was quite emotional. At the time of writing, we all still dress up and go in the Carnival. Our heritage carries on.

Great Grandfather Charles A Ward

14

In the fifties the Aldeburgh Music Festival was held at the Jubilee Hall across from us, and the whole town came alive and got involved with the festival. We always joked that when Richard was born on 17th June, 1957, that the flags were put up for him, but they were of course, the flags for the Festival.

A favourite festival pastime for Sarah, my great friend (who lived opposite at the Keys) and me, was to stand up at our bedroom windows at night and watch all the people and the excitement when they came to the Keys. Sarah started it one night, when she stood up at her bedroom window in her nightie and called, "Pat, Pat are you awake?" I soon replied that I was. I had a bunk bed and slept on top, so it was easy to look out of the window. We thought it amusing to see how the people were dressed, some in furs, others in black tails. Some men looked strange to us, with their hair being rather long standing on end and unbrushed. Maybe a conductor or two, Ha! We would giggle and play tricks, squirting water over them, or throw paper, and then hide. The bell would ring, and then off they would go back for the second half, as they'd been in the Keys having their drinks.

When the Festival Club was opened (by the Duke of Edinburgh in 1962) a few years later (on the corner facing the High Street opposite Ward's Garage and Crabbe Street) it gave us even more fun and excitement. They would play pop music and we got the occasional glimpse of the glamorous and famous actress, Sue Lloyd, whose family lived here, and one of her boyfriends Terrance Cooper, which was most exciting. Who could go off to sleep to the sounds of 'Rock around the Clock', but I would eventually get rocked off to sleep!

Early on in the Festival days a drummer and percussionist named James Blades came rushing into the Keys one night, asking if anyone could mend one of his drums as the skin was torn. Arthur Sheppard, the Landlord, said, "Try Brian Ward across the street". So he came knocking at our door. Dad said he could stitch it back for him and promptly mended the drum, so of course the show could carry on. From then on every year, while we lived there, that lovely man would pay us a visit, as he never forgot my Dad and his kindness. He always came and put coins in our hands and would stay and chat with us all. I loved his most wonderful smile and charming voice. He told us how he made special sound effects using containers with pebbles to simulate walking on the beach, etc. I thought of Mr Blades every time I watched the opening of a Rank film, which had the striking of the gong, because he made that sound. I was also fascinated by this man, as I heard he had run away as a child and joined a circus.

Through the Festival, somehow Mum and Dad became friends with some golfers. They would visit us, and on one occasion took Margaret who was about four or five years old, for a ride in their convertible silver Rolls-Royce. We never forgot the look on her face as she smiled and waved to everyone in town, as they took her around. We always joked it was "Princess Margaret".

Note: I have since discovered that one of my favourite actors, Michael Crawford, performed as a child in the Festival in "Noyes Fludde" at the Jubilee Hall. I wonder if our paths crossed in the street? I can remember peering backstage and looking at the fascinating make-up and costumes, maybe I had seen him there, but I will never know!

15

There were so many colourful characters living around us in those days. Many stand out as being the real Aldeburgh people, those who gave the town its charm and distinctiveness. Just in the hub of our little domain there were so many families, fishermen, business people and such. One such character was Miss Cragg of the Cragg Sisters Café, which was just a few doors away. She loved coming into the Keys in the evenings. You could hear her most distinct laugh echo loudly, as she sat in the Smoke Room, which was entered by a door opposite my bedroom window. Her laughter would ease me into the most blissful sleep. Miss Cragg went along to the Keys with Miss List quite often, as they were good friends and worked together in the café. Miss Cragg was so kind to us because we would often knock on her back door and ask for stale cakes, which she always had and would give us a bag full. I later became one of her waitresses (not a very good one, I might add) when I reached the age of thirteen.

Just around the corner into the High Street opposite the Town Steps was Timothy White's the chemist, which was there for many years. I loved Timothy White's because we had a most kind chemist, called Dr Watt, who was there for many years. He wasn't a real doctor of course, but oh, he had so many health

Dr Watt

tips for everyone if they enquired and everybody trusted him so well. One of his famous remarks in his strong Scottish accent was, "Thank God for good health, we've got a lot to be thankful for". I was thankful to him, because he so kindly gave me his lovely scented soapboxes, which I was always asking for to make dolls' beds. He let me stand in the shop for hours on end, sampling and looking at all the cosmetics and he never seemed to mind. He got to know us all in the town so well.

Next door (No.31) we had Mrs Phil Bickerton, who lived alone and owned numerous cats. She lived there the whole time we did, so we knew her well. She had a nice cottage garden and I loved to look in. Sometimes she cooked for Miss Cragg; I noticed her strength in supporting herself (she and I later worked for the Labour tote round and she was a dedicated worker).

Next door at No.27 lived an elderly lady (name unknown) and I believe it was sort of a holiday home. She used to let her daughter and her family come and use it. Luckily for me the two eldest children were around my age, Annabelle and Sebastian (Sebby), who was my first love at the age of six. I thought him so handsome, and I had my very first kiss with him down on the 'rec'.

Behind the Keys near the sea front were two real strong Aldeburgh families, which have lived on. One was the Baggott family, who owned the nearby newsagents. Jack lived there with his wife and children. He was a spry fellow with a wonderful full moustache and was an industrious worker. (His brother Lorrie also worked in town.) I loved his Baggott's shop, not because of the sweets or buckets and spades, but because of his warm welcome every time I went in which must have been every day of my life, while living down there. The town still has a Baggott's Newsagents to this day. so the name lives on!

Jack Baggott

Next door to the Baggott family were 'Rats' Mower and wife Freda, plus six children. Rats, a fisherman, was a warm, beautiful man. He was always tanned, always smiling and always out on the beach. In his large family, some were friends of mine, especially Carol (see Carnival photo) and Pip who looked a lot like her father. She was a lot of fun. Rats wore gold earrings, which always fascinated me. Later I came to find out from Dad that if a fisherman wore gold earrings he would have enough money from them to pay for a burial if drowned at sea. A photo of Rats was hung in the Keys and stayed there into 2005.

'Rats' Mower

Next door to the Keys lived the Prevettes. The family owned the Church Farm, a dairy farm. They had two daughters about my age, Elizabeth and Linda, the younger of the two I played with primarily. I often visited their house, which was a large property facing the sea front. For a period of time in the front they had a popular café called the 'Copper Jug'.

Down the street, opposite the Jubilee Hall were two tiny cottages (since demolished) where two families lived and had children my age. One family was called Mower, Dudley and wife Dulce, with Cliffy (nickname) their son. Next door was the Burns family, Bob and Doris and their son Rodney who was my age and in my class at school. We all played together. Later the boys both became fishermen and good ones too!

Further down in the opposite direction in Oakley Square lived the Bridel family, with their two daughters Pat and Carol, with whom I played. In Oakley Square next door to the Copper Jug lived the Lye family, whose youngest daughter Caroline was a friend. Her sister Copper married an American G.I. who was particularly kind to me, when I was in hospital aged ten having an eye operation. He bought me the biggest, softest cuddly bear, when I came home, I felt so lucky with my American Bear.

Sharing our back yard wall was another Ward family; Dad's cousin Ron lived there with his wife Vera and two sons, David and Stephen. The front of their house faced Ward's Garage, Grandad's old garage (where Dad was born in the back at Pine Cottage, since demolished). I visited their house all the time and we were always playing in their backyard, ours being too small. We were all close. (See photo of all of us children at their house in 1958). Vera (after we left in 1967), sadly died when the boys were young, which was hurtful for us all.

Children at play
left to right: Eunice Measures, Phillip Linsell, (baby unknown), the Ward Clan (all cousins) Susan, Pat, Richard, Paula, Michael, Stephen, David and Margaret.

These were just a few of the families that lived near us, so I was never without friends to play with. Some other characters that made an impression on me, who lived in other parts of town, will stay with me forever. One well-known character of the town was 'Sunny' Collis, who often visited us. He was a wild, charming man, very well liked, but he loved to drink. He was Dad's friend and they spent many a Sunday lunchtime together, having midday refreshments in the local pubs. Dad would kindly invite Sunny to our house on these occasions, after closing time. Often tables and chairs would get in Sunny' way, it was a small house, after all! He was a strong man with a lovely manner, and was a fisherman at one point. He loved us children.

Sunny Collis and Wally Fisher

Another character in town who made an impression on me as a young child was Miss Percy Smith, a dedicated Christian lady. She was a faithful servant to those in need. I had a spell of a few months in the Cottage Hospital when I was about six years old. She came there nearly every day to visit and went out shopping for the patients who needed things. Since I was there for observation, she took me along with her. We would go hand in hand down the town to the shops and she also took me to her lovely house just opposite the tennis courts. She was an environmentalist even then, as her house was full of items to recycle, so many egg boxes! I really admired her dedication to the Lord's work and I'll never forget her kindness to me.

A real comic of a character was Bill Ewer. He dressed up in the Carnival year after year in so many comical outfits and preceded Mum and Dad in that role. We all looked out for him in the Carnival, with his friend Felix Thorpe. I loved his daring nature as he just gave it his all. He made the Carnival something special for child or adult, maybe a reason for some of the Carnival's popularity. These characters of Aldeburgh made my childhood something special and there were so many more, too many to mention. How lucky was Aldeburgh!

Bill Ewer and Felix Thorpe

16

I was fortunate enough to have the most freedom loving play in those days. Since we didn't have a garden (just a tiny yard), the beach became my playground. Right by the two lifeboats there were poles in the beach, which supported ropes that went right down into the sea. I could climb on to the poles and do tightrope walking quite high up and the ropes in the sea were great for hanging on to while splashing feet. On the higher ropes, I was always hanging upside down, I could have joined a circus after that! The steps to the beach had handrails, and these too I would use to climb and hang on or slide down. It was great fun. Dad (whose family were excellent swimmers) used to swim right out to sea once a year to the buoy, when he got there he would wave, we would all stand waving back. I was very proud of him.

Sarah and I lived in the sea, like mermaids we were. We used the metal groins to jump off into the sea. All our childhood days were spent on the beach. Her mother, Joan, saved me from drowning once, when I was about four years old, but I was never scared of the sea, I loved it. One funny thing happened with the sea. Margaret had a little metal pram, which had a loose cranky wheel and would make such a noise, you knew when she was coming. She loved her pram, but Dad got a bit frustrated with the noise and it was beyond repair, so he decided to discard it in the sea (often this happened to things in those days). He didn't tell Margaret and of course she kept looking and looking for her pram and missed it greatly. Then a few days later, while we were all playing on the water's edge, (Richard, Margaret and I) all of a sudden a huge wave came up and much to our amazement the little pram got washed up too. Margaret brought it home, even squeakier than ever!

I loved the beach, but my favourite place to play was down near the river. Down there were huge concrete blocks, which had been used for war defences. These made great places to make little houses, each block was used for a room, down further another child would have his or her house, so you could visit. It was amazing how long you could play there without getting bored, with only a few tin cans and sticks to cook with. I loved it there in summer and would spend all day long there, only coming home for meal times.

Further down was the derelict Martello Tower. What excitement could be had there. We could climb in through an open window that faced the sea, and climb along narrow wooden beams (with nails sticking out in places) and below was a long drop down to the dungeon. How brave I felt climbing across to the stairs. Once you got up to the top, what a view, it was marvellous. There were pieces of gunnery metal, which had been used in the war, to play with. All the children of Aldeburgh would meet there, especially the boys, and tomboy girls like me.

Also down the river was the old boat called the 'Ionia' which was a landmark stuck in the mud. It was used, I had heard, for orphan children to have holidays in at one time but I'm not 100% sure. That was before my time and was abandoned when I played there. It was a great place to play.

Down that part of town the 'Fair' would come at Carnival time, as it still does, and it was the highlight of the year to go down with my friends and I'd go every night. I loved the fair, with its excitement and still do.

I was, at one point in a gang, who were mostly boys, the only other girl who sometimes came along was Jenny Keeble, another tomboy, who was unafraid. I loved our gang, we were do-gooders, we tried to stick up for the underdog. The gang leader was Anthony Knowles, a very good-looking blond- headed boy, who I had a crush on (his father was Major at the time). Paul McMullin, who lived down towards Fort Green, was another member, a level headed boy with a good nature; he was Anthony's right-hand man. We would ride bikes around town and we would make dens down on Dad's marsh by the river. Every day with the 'gang' was an adventure.

I often played with my good friends John and Ann Fisher, who lived at the bottom of the small steps, West Lane, with parents Wally and Mary. John was a handsome boy a couple of years my junior, but I believe I had a soft spot for him. I played with them quite a bit at their house, and on the beach. Wally was one of Dad's friends too, and Mary being Irish fitted in nicely with our family. Right near their house on the High Street, would often be a vehicle counter man who would sit in a little hut all day marking. I would often chat to the man. I think he liked my little visits which I would do after visiting John and Ann.

Just on the High Street nearby lived Trevor Harvey, whose parents kept the fishmongers. We were in the same class and we got on particularly well up in the art room. Trevor later became involved with the Carnival, and has done so to the present day.

Carol Strowger, also in my class at school, lived down the south end of the High Street and we were friends right through our teenage years. Carol was a good loyal friend, quiet in nature but she also had a spark for a laugh. We played her dear mum Eileen up many a time when I visited their house. I would go to watch TV since we didn't own one. We loved watching 'The Lone Ranger'. Keith, Carol's brother would play with us too. Their father, Arthur, had been a fisherman. Eileen was a wonderful lady who came from Surrey, her accent then was quite unusual to hear in those days. How she put up with us, I will never know. She was a Deacon at my Baptist Church and a dedicated Christian.

Talking of the Baptist Church, I attended Sunday school there for many years. Mr Barker was our teacher and he lived next door to the Fishers on the small steps. He continued to be involved with the church until his death, at over ninety years of age. He loved the children greatly, and we him.

On my first day at school, I met and became friends with Linda Barnes she was an up town girl, but we hit it off. Our friendship continued right through our teenage years. Carol, Linda and I were, 'Hear no evil', 'See no evil' and 'Speak no evil'!

Lastly, one of my special friends was an American girl named Margaret Howard who lived in Lee Road near the school. Her father of course was at RAF Bentwaters, her mother was German. I loved Margaret because for those days, she was a liberated girl. She was a bit younger than me, but we got on like a house on fire. She could get away with a lot (she was another sort of tomboy) because she said what she thought. She liked the boys and would tease them. I used to try and copy her tactics.

Dad told me that one day she came and played outside our house with some children. She supposedly wasn't allowed to, and her father came and beat her in the street in front of everyone (luckily I wasn't there at the time), but it really upset my father.

I'll never forget one day when she came to my house on her bike, and said she was going to run away from home and asked if I'd come with her. I can remember saying, "Yes, I'll come, things haven't been too good lately, for me either". So off we went, with one bike between us. We got as far as Thorpeness and had to call at the first house to ask for a drink of water. When we knocked on the door and a lady answered, she asked us what we were doing, so we told her we were running away from home. So she said, "If I give you the water, will you promise you will go home"? As we were thirsty, we said, "Yes", and promptly set off back! Note: Years later in my teens I managed to trace Margaret in the States and we wrote to each other, which was great.

Dad was good at making things and he made me wooden stilts, which were quite high, and these were great fun, along with the treacle tin versions! Our play was simple, but fun. The hours with the hula-hoop amounted to thousands.

Part of my summer I would go and stay at my aunt Joan (Dad's sister) and Ted's house in Ipswich. Joan was exceedingly sporty, as were her two children Angela and Derek (champion swimmers for Suffolk). So I loved going there, as she would take me to Broom Hill outdoor swimming pool where she helped me with my swimming. She also taught me so many things such as sewing and gardening. It was like being at a finishing school. I was like a rough stone, and she polished me till I shone on the inside and out. I loved her.

Lastly our relatives would come from Stoke-on-Trent (Mum's sister Lovey and her husband George) to camp on Dad's marsh in the summer time. They would bring another family with them who had loads of children. So we would have a bonfire in the evening with singing and dancing which would go on through the night. It was very gypsy like, but oh, the fun.

My playtime was simple but oh, so memorable. I think I was lucky.

Class Six in 61.
Left Helen Alexander, Pat, Jane Hollister and Carol Strowger

17

My mother's grandparents were the Bacons, who came from Yoxford. When Nana Bacon was in her nineties she caught pneumonia and had to go into the Aldeburgh Cottage Hospital, Grandad 'Winkles' stayed at our house so he could easily visit his wife. At the time Nana Bacon was in there, Mum told us that when she arrived at the Hospital, she said to the doctor, "I can't be staying in here, I've got my canning and pickling to do" And she did too! I always remembered Grandad as 'Rasher', but have since learned that was his brother's name, how 'Rasher' stuck I don't know.

Winkles was short in stature, and had problems with his legs. I can remember Dad carrying him on his back up the stairs, it was a comical sight, and I would stand and watch. Later, I have been told that on one occasion as they were going up stairs one of them got his foot caught in a trouser leg cuff and they went tumbling down, but Dad managed to keep hold of him and caught him safely at the bottom. Winkles had the most ancient of Suffolk accents and would often say to me, if I was playfully teasing Margaret, "Will you stopa plaguing har"!

18

Dad being a carpenter and builder decided to alter and improve our house, as I have mentioned. It took many years to do. He had to do as much as he could afford, so he couldn't do it all at once, and time was a factor. He eventually created a bathroom upstairs (we had no bathroom at all) with a toilet. In spite of my mother's appeal it did take a long time. When he took out the stairs he needed a ceiling support in the kitchen and put a beam in, which was a slip for launching the lifeboat and we are not sure if the tar was still on it, but it wouldn't surprise me. We also think the bottom stair was made out of a fish crate off the beach. When Dad took the stairs out and built a new section at the back of the house he found out (with a nasty shock) that when trying to put the old stairs in through the roof they didn't fit as they were two inches too big. His measurements were correct for the bottom of the original part of the house, but he didn't realise the top wasn't 'plumb'. But with a bit of sanding and manoeuvring he managed to get them in, single handed I might add.

One of the things that I will never forget was that Dad had to renew the kitchen floor and dug out the whole area which was completely a bed of soil. He was digging away (near the front door) and suddenly dropped down several feet and was saved by his elbows! He had found a large hole. He looked rather funny down there. At the bottom he cleared a bit and discovered there was a tunnel that went right in the direction of the Keys. Maybe it was a smuggler's tunnel, we will never know. I took some of the cragg to show the children at school. It was quite a find. Dad now tells me that the whole area has shingle underneath the ground and is affected by the tides.

With all the work going on it was hard for Mum, with all of us children. It wasn't easy. For me, I always had rough hands from going up and down the stairs touching the cinder blocks. We had to have a laugh and see the funny side of things. Before the house was finished a funny thing happened when we had a hard snowy winter. Dad cleared a path of snow not to the shops but across to the Keys. He got his priorities right!

19

Our house was always filled with music usually from Radio Luxembourg or records Mum borrowed from Jill Strowger and her American friends, mostly Country and Western music. There were many parties held, sometimes to my displeasure if I was woken up by the music. The house had real life. Mum's brother Peter Murphy and his best friend 'Rampy' Thurston used to visit our house all the time, they loved a night out in Aldeburgh because it was well known for the night life. They were a great pair: Peter had a very fun outgoing personality to say the least, and Rampy was a quieter chap who had a subtle sense of humour. Peter was the front man, always a joker and Rampy came up behind, but they made a fun team. They were very stylish in dress and hair. Teddy Boys in the true sense of the word! Every time they went to the Jubilee Hall dances, entering they would say, "P.M and R.T.", and just walk straight in without paying!

One of the most exciting and fascinating things that I observed was the arrival on a Saturday night of the Murphy girls (Mum's sisters). They would call in on their way to the dances at the Jubilee Hall. Auntie Josie would come with her friends, who would come down on the bus from Leiston and taxi home. My eyes must have been so wide when they would arrive because what struck me was their glamour and dark gently teased hair. The beauty was amazing (Dad always said the Murphy girls were renowned throughout Suffolk). Their clothes were so stylish and they would wear tight-waisted skirts with wasbie belts around their smallest of waists. High-heeled shoes were worn and seamed stockings were the rage then too, red lipstick and you get the picture. I envied them going off to the dances and couldn't wait for my turn. It didn't take too long and came when I was around twelve years old. I was allowed to go and stay till 9.30 p.m.

On one of my first dances, someone kindly pointed out to me that my brother and sister were there. There were dear Margaret and Richard standing together sweetly smiling and looking so pleased to be there too! Promptly, out of embarrassment I told them to go straight home. I got over that and spent the rest of my teenage years going to the dances every Saturday night. It was usually dancing to the Leiston band, called the 'Rebels' and later called the 'Wild Oats', and I loved every number they played. I have a lot to thank that band for, because they gave me such a marvellous youthful time.

On 14th October, 1961, the second home birth took place at No. 29. Dear Elizabeth Jane (Lizzy), the fourth child of our family was born and she was a beautiful child.

20

In those days we were very lucky to have what I call everyday shops in the town. There were at least four excellent butcher shops. Two main hardware stores were with us for so many years, Beeches being one, the other Constances. Hallas was a fantastic fruit and vegetable shop, which must have run over fifty years from father to son. We were also lucky to have two very good toyshops in town, one which sold bikes (where I got my first bike), and we had two homemade baker shops, two fish and chip shops. One of my favourite shops was Freeman Hardy and Willis shoes (the shop was once owned by my Ward great grandparents). I passed it every day as it was at the end of Crabbe Street, where I bought my first 'winkle picker' shoes. I loved that shop. Next to Timothy Whites on the High Street was a curiosity and antique shop. Inside it had a hundred and one clocks, all ticking at the same time! I loved going in. I don't know who it belonged to in early times, but later Ronny Ashford owned it. O & C Butcher also did groceries and owned a shop at the south end of town near the Black Horse pub (since closed) and they had another shop up on Victoria Road (now a house). We had three garages in town. The first one, Ward & Son, opened in the 1920's by my Great-grandfather Charles A, when there were only two cars in the town! It was a garage for over 90 years (see photo). We had five hotels, The East Suffolk on the High Street was run for many years by my Great grand father Charles A. starting in 1890's. We really didn't have to travel out of town for anything, as the town supplied all our needs. And of course we had all the fish we needed off of the beach! I was lucky to live in the old Aldeburgh!

6   In 1933 it was a bumper year for herrings in which my Grandfather Charles E. was involved with. My great, great uncle George W. Ward formed a quartet of Aldeburgh fishermen who sent annually the first catch of the season to

the late King Edward and Queen's banquet table. He owned the bathing machines and fishing boats which he rented out to fishermen who couldn't afford their own boats. To read more about this amazing man see 'Clifford' by Pamela Blackburn, Optima Press, Osborn Park, WA. (in Suffolk Libraries).

Ward's Garage in the 1930's.
Grandfather Charles E. standing, who ran it until late 1930's.
Note: the petrol pump on the pavement, it was there until the garage closed, some 90 years later!

East Suffolk Hotel approximately 1894. Grandfather Charlie E in pram with his parents. Great grandfather ran the hotel for many years and used horse carriages to pick up passengers at the station and then later used a Ford bus and he also ran a service to Thorpeness.

21

Our Little House had suddenly become overcrowded. There were three children in one bedroom, where Margaret and I topped and toed in the top bunk bed and Richard was below. So my parents knew the time had come when we would have to leave Little House in Crabbe Street No.29, and move to a bigger house. It took a couple of years to happen. First the house had to be completed and then they had to save for new things, furniture, etc. So it didn't happen straight away. The house was sold for £1,850.00 in 1963!

I can remember that when it was time to go I couldn't move. I stayed a while longer with the Prevetts. I made a fuss of the new décor of my bedroom and made them change it. So I stayed down longer as I just didn't want to leave Crabbe Street. In the end I had to go and went very reluctantly. Is there any wonder, because the time living in 29 Crabbe Street was so fantastic, the life in that street was amazing. It was early 1963 that I moved into 19 Franklin Road and that's another story!

THE END

Richard's drawing of Crabbe Street
Back of Cragg Sisters Café and Timothy White's Chemist
One of Richard's first drawings 1973 (aged 16)

Children's Christmas Party, approximately 1958 at the East Suffolk Hotel. We regularly had these parties held by the R.O.A.B. the "Buffs". (Pat bottom left, mum with baby Richard top right) Great grandfather Charles A. was one of its founders of the "George Crabbe" Lodge in 1913.

High Street, 1955
Copyright The Francis Frith Collection, SP35QP © www.francisfrith.com

Crabbe Street, 1955 - No 29 on left
Copy Wright Francis Frith Collection, SP35QP © www.francisfrith.com

The Aldeburgh lifeboat Abdy Beauclerk being launched in 1957 to take part in the first co-ordinated exercise with an RAF helicopter. The second Aldeburgh boat, Lucy Lavers is in the background. The crew on that day were John Burrell, Horace Sharman, Bob Smith, Ron Ward, Maurice Smith and Brian Ward

L to R   CLASS 6 - 1961

Back Row: Peter Pearce, Fred Churchyard, Andrew Cutler, Jane Hollister, Linda Barnes, Michael Hardman, Pat Knights, Timothy Eaves, Richard Warren, Haydn Cook, Helen Alexander, Trevor Harvey, Peter Moss, David Tiffin, ?, Fred Carter, Nicholas Penny, Joan Cook, Rodney Burns, David McMullan, Julie Wells, Carol Strowger, Miss Steven, Pat Ward, Jennifer Keable, David McCullan, John Bethel, ? Cooper, Robin Wigg, John Thorpe, Jimmy White, Simon Ovens

Ionia sketch by Richard 1971 moored on the River Alde for many years but the following year was burned down by the Town Council.

Photos of Carnivals Past and Present

Grandmother Florence Ward, 1930's, outside Pine Cottage
(back of Ward's Garage) since demolished.

Dad, Richard The Clown, Mum and Margaret

Mum and Dad as Gazzarotti and Pavarotti

Mum and Dad as Ken Dodd and The Diddy Man

Lizzy and Dad - Pixie Power

Resting on Our Laurels - Dad and Mum
(used their bed)

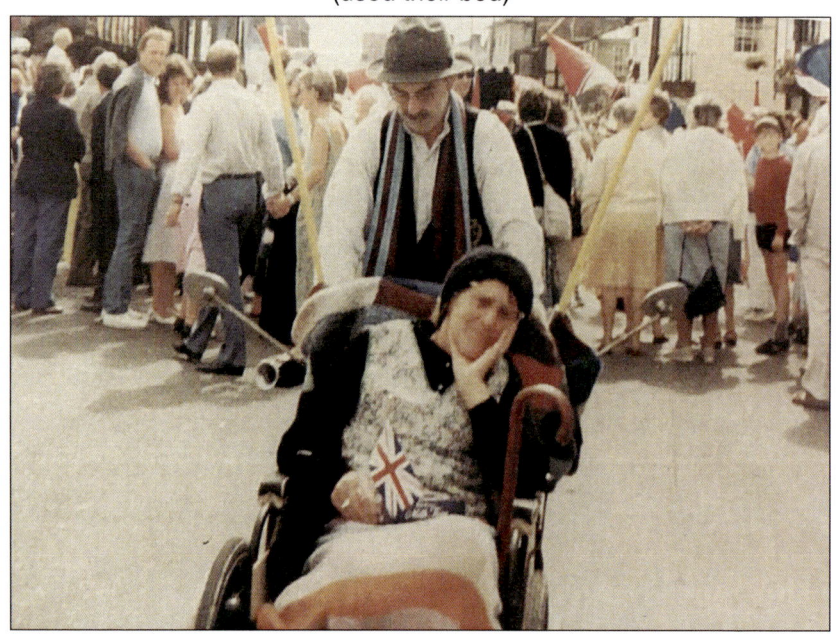

Mum & Dad - Alf Garnet and his Silly Ol Moo

Mum and Dad as Michael Jackson and Bubbles the chimp 1988

Son Nick in Four and Twenty Blackbirds late 1980s

'Pat the Sprat' 2015
written on her backside
'Our Heritage'

Pearly Kings and Queens 2007
Pat, Dad, friend Lauren and Lizzy's Nathan

Pat and Sarah, 'The two Charlie Chaplins', coincidently,
we dressed the same, 2019.

"All dressed up and no carnival"
Pat outside Carnival Cottage August 17th 2020
(wearing an old carnival outfit)

EPILOGUE

Margaret later went on to own an Art Gallery – The Aldeburgh Gallery in the High Street and stilldoes.

Richard became an Artist and exhibited often in Margaret's gallery. He died at the age of 39.

Elizabeth (Lizzy) lives in Leiston with her husband and has three children.

Colleen and Brian (Mum and Dad) were a comedy pair always performing In the Aldeburgh Carnival. Colleen died in 1998. Brian (nicknamed 'Pixie' since a child) and performed in the Carnival till 89 years old, he died in 2018.

Sarah (best friend) still goes in the Carnival, often with the Wards and lives in Aldeburgh.

Jonathan the youngest child (who does not appear in the book) was born in 1967 and lives in Kesgrave.

Pat Now retired (Nursery Teacher). I enjoy singing and dancing with 'The Pearlies' variety show in which dad was involved for many years.